Dedicated to the loving children of the Heart of God Orphanage
in Port au Prince, Haiti. I keep your lessons most preciously.

People of the Bible
Copyright © 2004 Scandinavia
This edition published 2005 by Authentic Media,
Milton Keynes, MK1 1QR, UK
Text © 2004 Leyah Jensen
Illustrations © 2004 José Pérez Montero
Design by Ben Alex   Printed in China
ISBN 1-86024-541-2

PEOPLE OF THE
BIBLE

Text by Leyah Jensen
Illustrations by José Pérez Montero

Authentic

Contents

Adam & Eve *Genesis 1:1–3:24*

In the beginning, there was nothing but darkness.

There was no water and no land, no animals and no people. But in the silence, there was God. God had a plan. "Let there be light!" He said. Suddenly, the blackness lit up in shining gold.

God separated the light from the darkness. He called the light day, and the darkness night. Then God stretched space deep and wide. He placed the planets and the stars in the sky. He created water and land on earth, with plants to grow.

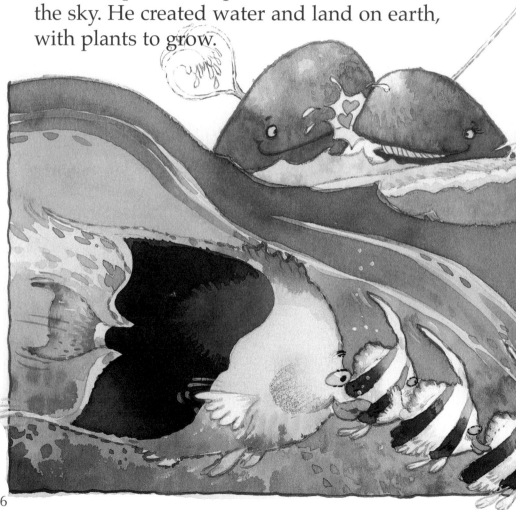

God filled the oceans with fish of amazing shapes and colours. "Be fruitful and multiply," He told them.

God made birds to fly overhead. Then He made animals of every kind to live on land. Some creatures were large and some were small. Some were spiky, and some were soft.

9

God had one last
creation—people!
God made a man, and
named him Adam.

He made a woman,
and named her Eve.
Adam and Eve loved
each other very much.

Together, they gave names to
God's creations.

God told Adam and Eve to take
good care of the animals. Then
they all lived together peacefully in
the beautiful garden called Eden,
feeling God's love everywhere!

God provided for all their needs. They could eat any fruit they wanted…except the fruit from the tree in the middle of the garden. One day, an evil snake tricked them into eating it anyway.

Adam and Eve knew that they had sinned. They became afraid, and tried to hide.

16

Yet God can see everywhere, and found them. When He learned that they had disobeyed, God was very, very sad. He sent them away from the garden, to never return. From now on they would have to work hard and grow their own food. Adam and Eve never felt as close to God again.

Cain & Abel

Adam and Eve made a home for themselves outside of the garden. Soon Eve gave birth to a baby, and named him Cain. Then they had a second son and named him Abel.

God loved their family very much.
He watched out for them, seeing all
that happened.

19

Cain and Abel each had a special job.
Abel took care of the animals,
while Cain took care of the fields.

Both Cain and
Abel loved God.

21

They each wanted to
give God a gift.

Cain gave God some of the crops from his
harvest. But Abel gave God his best lamb.
When God saw the gifts, He was happier
with Abel's gift than Cain's. This made
Cain very jealous of his brother.

Cain told Abel to come out into the field with him. Then, Cain attacked his brother and killed him!

Since God sees everything, He knew what Cain had done. God was so angry that He sent Cain away from home, telling him that he would never be able to grow anything again.

But it's never too late to ask for forgiveness. Even after the terrible thing Cain had done, God kept him from harm and gave him a family of his own.

A long time passed...

Adam and Eve had a descendant named Noah, who loved God with all his heart.

But the rest of the world had stopped listening to God. People were violent and sinful. God was so unhappy that He decided to start again with just one family—Noah's.

God said to Noah, "Get ready!" God was going to send a flood to cover the whole earth.

God told Noah to build an enormous boat of strong wood—one hundred and fifty metres long! The boat should also have many floors with many rooms, and a big door in the side. He should put a roof on the top. People came from far around to laugh at Noah as he worked away. After all…

…*Noah was building a boat in the desert!*

When the boat was at last finished, God told Noah to gather every kind of animal. Two by two, Noah and his family loaded them into the boat. They divided the animals into the different rooms.

31

Noah and his family went into the
boat last, and closed the door. Then
it began to rain, and rain…and rain!
The ocean filled up and the sky
poured down. The earth flooded
for forty days and forty nights.

God did not
forget faithful Noah.
At last the rain stopped
and the waves became
still. Noah sent a
raven to find dry land,
but the bird came back.

No dry
land yet!

Noah sent out a dove. The dove also came back, so everyone waited in the boat. When Noah sent out the dove a second time, it brought back a leaf. The earth was drying up!

The third time, the dove did not come
back. Noah knew that it was time!
He opened the roof of the boat…

...and then, when God commanded,
Noah opened the door!
The animals were overjoyed to be
on land again.

39

Noah and his family were grateful too. Everyone praised God. Then Noah built an altar, where he gave God gifts to thank Him for keeping them safe.

God had made a new world!

Then God made three promises to Noah. The first promise was that there would always be seasons...

...*summer, autumn, winter, and spring.*

43

God also said that there would always be night and day. His last promise was that He would never again flood the whole earth. To make sure that people never forgot this promise…

...*God placed a beautiful rainbow in the sky!*

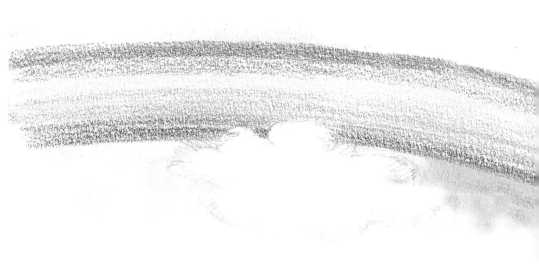

Noah and his family began to make a new home. God blessed them, and they had many children and grandchildren.

Rainbows reminded the people that God's love is gigantic, and never has an end!

Abraham

Genesis 12:1–22:18

After a while, some people forgot about
God and His promises. But not Abraham.
He served God faithfully in all he did.

49

Abraham did as God told him. He set off with his wife Sarah on the long journey to a new land. God kept them safe and strong. He also blessed them with riches...

...and gave them many animals—goats, sheep, and camels!

Abraham and Sarah travelled day after day through the hot desert. They knew that God was leading them. It was dry and dusty, but God gave them water.

Abraham always remembered to stop and thank God for loving them so much.

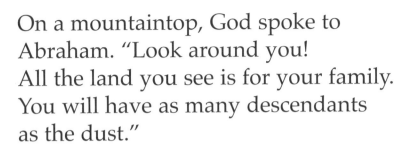

On a mountaintop, God spoke to
Abraham. "Look around you!
All the land you see is for your family.
You will have as many descendants
as the dust."

*When it grew dark,
God said, "Look at the sky!
You will have as many
descendants as the stars."*

God gave Abraham and Sarah a
beautiful boy. They named him Isaac.
One day God told Abraham to take
Isaac up to a hilltop. He
wanted Abraham to give Isaac
back to Him.

Abraham was very sad. He loved his son Isaac, and didn't want to give him up. But since God was the most important part of his life, he decided to obey.

Early the next morning, Abraham took Isaac and set off. When they got to the place that God had instructed, Abraham built an altar and laid Isaac on top. But right before Abraham was about to kill Isaac, a voice came from heaven!

"Don't hurt the boy!" said the Angel of the Lord. "Now you have proven your faith, because you were willing to give up your precious son. But God does not want the boy to die."

Abraham was very grateful—he loved Isaac more than anything on earth! Abraham thanked God for saving the boy's life.

God promised to protect Abraham and his family for a long time to come. The whole world would be blessed, because Abraham obeyed God!

Sarah

Genesis 18:1–21:7

Isaac was such a big blessing to Abraham and Sarah, because they almost thought he would never arrive!

When they started getting old, they still had no children. But through all their journeys, they believed that God would give them the big family He had promised. They had to have at least one baby if they were going to have as many descendants as stars in the sky!

63

Yet it got harder and harder to keep believing. Sarah was now over ninety years old!

One day, three strangers came to visit. Sarah and her servants prepared their very best food. Abraham stood nearby as they ate, realizing that the visitors were sent from God!

Sarah was listening inside the tent when one of the visitors spoke. He said that Sarah would soon have a baby.

Sarah laughed right out loud.
How could an old lady have a baby?

The visitor said, "Why did Sarah laugh? Nothing is impossible for God."

Sure enough, Sarah soon had a baby boy! They named him Isaac. Sarah was very happy, and praised God for His wonderful gift. She had waited a long time…but God always keeps His promises.

Sarah said, "God has brought me laughter, and everyone who hears about this will laugh with me!"

Abraham and Sarah lived long and joyful lives, with Isaac as the beginning of the enormous family God had promised. Isaac would grow up to marry Rebekah, and they would have many children. Those children would also have many children.

73

Joseph

Genesis 37:1–46:12

Isaac had a son
named Jacob, and
Jacob had twelve
sons of his own.
Joseph was Jacob's
favourite son.

Jacob gave him a beautiful coat. When Joseph's brothers saw that their father loved him more than them, they became jealous.

Joseph would often have strange dreams when he was asleep.

One night, he dreamt that he was ruler. The sun, moon, and eleven stars bowed down to him! When he told his brothers about the dream, they laughed. "Do you really think you will rule over us?" Now they hated Joseph more than ever.

The brothers made a plan to get rid of
Joseph. When he came to check on them
in the fields, they grabbed him and took
his special robe.

Then they threw him into an empty well. Some of the brothers thought he should be killed, but soon they had a better idea.

Before long, a caravan of merchants passed the place where the brothers were eating. The brothers pulled Joseph out of the well, and sold him to the merchants for silver.

The merchants were going to take Joseph to Egypt, as a slave!

Yet God stayed right by Joseph's side...
even when he was sold to a captain in
Egypt. Joseph worked very hard, and was
good at everything he did. His master
saw that God blessed Joseph, so he put
Joseph in charge of all he owned.

His master's wife started to like Joseph. Joseph told her that this was wrong. She became so angry that she lied to her husband about bad things that Joseph had done.

The captain believed his wife, and had Joseph thrown in jail. The Lord stayed with Joseph even in jail, though. One day two of the prisoners each had a dream. With God's help, Joseph interpreted the dreams to tell the men what they meant.

The prisoners were very grateful for Joseph's help.

Two years later, Pharaoh, the King of Egypt, had a dream. None of his magicians or wise men could tell him what it meant. Then he learned about Joseph, and brought him out of jail to hear the dream. Joseph told Pharaoh that the dream meant there was a famine ahead, and he had to get ready by saving food.

Pharaoh was so thankful for the meaning of his dream, that he made Joseph like a king himself! "I hereby put you in charge of the whole land of Egypt," Pharaoh said.

Seven years later came the drought that Joseph had predicted, ruining lands far and wide. Away in Canaan, his father and brothers were hungry. Jacob told his sons, "I hear that there is grain in Egypt. Go there and buy some for us, so that we won't starve."

The brothers departed with silver in their sacks to buy food.

The brothers arrived in Egypt. They
came before Joseph to ask for food, not
recognizing that he was their brother
whom they had sold as a slave. Joseph,
though, recognized them at once. When
he saw his youngest brother Benjamin,
he hid tears of happiness.

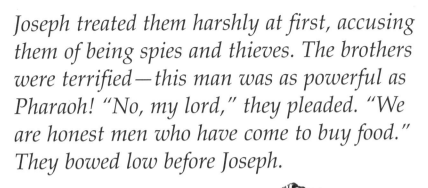

Joseph treated them harshly at first, accusing them of being spies and thieves. The brothers were terrified—this man was as powerful as Pharaoh! "No, my lord," they pleaded. "We are honest men who have come to buy food." They bowed low before Joseph.

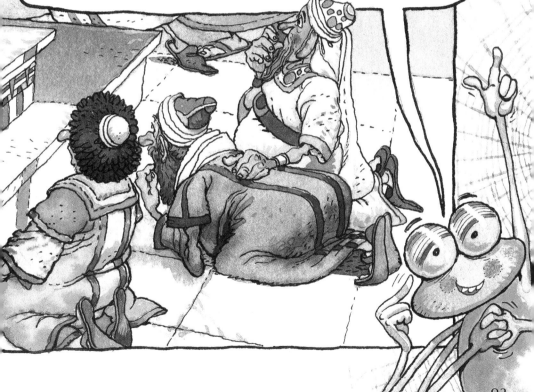

Finally Joseph could keep his secret no longer. "I am Joseph!" he cried out. When they came closer, they could see that it was true. "Don't be angry with yourselves for having sold me as a slave," he said. "It was part of God's plan, so that our family would not starve when the famine came!"

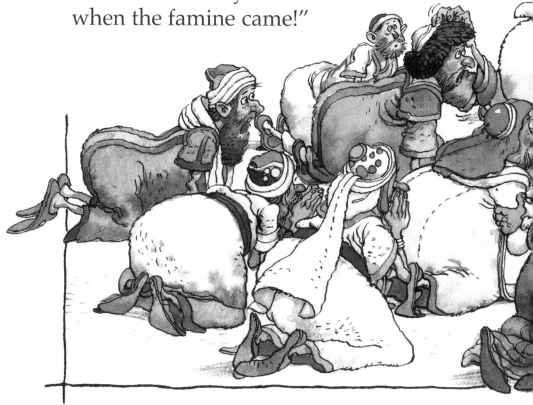

Joseph had forgiven them for the cruel things they had done to him.

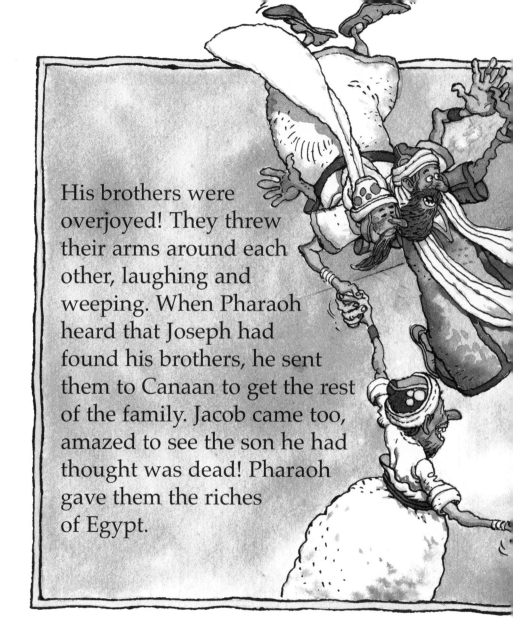

His brothers were overjoyed! They threw their arms around each other, laughing and weeping. When Pharaoh heard that Joseph had found his brothers, he sent them to Canaan to get the rest of the family. Jacob came too, amazed to see the son he had thought was dead! Pharaoh gave them the riches of Egypt.

They all lived happily together in Egypt for the rest of their days—never to go hungry again! Jacob's descendants were called Israelites, and their numbers grew and grew.

Moses

Exodus 1:6–20:17

Long after Joseph had lived, a bad
Pharaoh ruled Egypt. He didn't like
how many Israelites there were in
Egypt, so he forced them to become
slaves. Then he ordered his soldiers
to kill the Israelite babies.

99

Sure enough, the princess herself saw the basket. She took the baby out of the river, and named him Moses. He became her son.

Moses grew up in the Pharaoh's palace, just like a real prince.

101

Yet Moses knew that he was an
Israelite. It made him sad to see how
the Egyptians mistreated his people.
One day he saw an Egyptian hitting an
Israelite. When no one was looking…

...Moses killed the Egyptian. Pharaoh came after him, so Moses ran away.

103

Moses settled in a new land…though
God had not forgotten His plan for him.
While Moses was tending his sheep,
God spoke to him from a burning bush!
God said that He wanted Moses to go and
rescue the Israelites from the Egyptians.

Moses wasn't so sure.

God promised to send miracles in order to show everyone that He had sent Moses. Moses obeyed God and journeyed back to Egypt. "Let my people go!" he said to Pharaoh.

Pharaoh refused to free the Israelites. Instead, he made the work even harder for them. God punished the Egyptians for this. First He made their water go bad...

Then He sent insects, sickness, and storms! When many Egyptians died, Pharaoh at last changed his mind.

The Israelites gathered their belongings and hurried off towards the desert. The Lord sent a cloud to guide them by day, and a pillar of fire to guide them by night. When they came to the sea, Moses stretched out his hand. Then God parted the water, so that there was a path of dry ground! Moses and all the Israelites crossed between the walls of water, to safety.

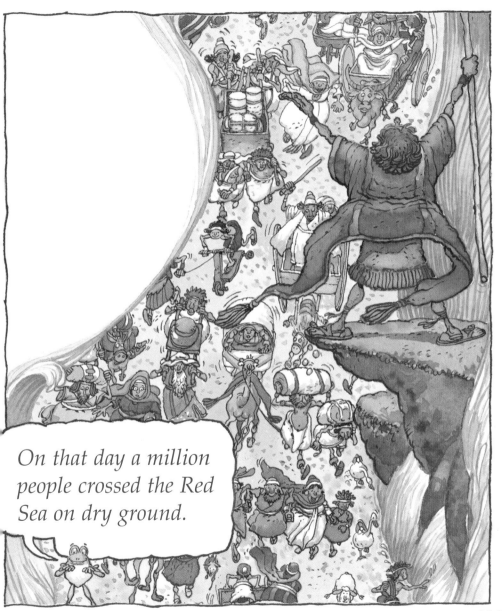

On that day a million people crossed the Red Sea on dry ground.

Pharaoh soon regretted that he had lost all of his slaves, and sent his soldiers after the Israelites. But when Pharaoh's army tried to cross the parted sea, God sent the walls of water crashing down on them! His whole army drowned.

Moses and the Israelites sang their thanks to God. They lived in the desert, and God gave them food and water. It wasn't always easy to trust God—soon the people began to grumble. God decided to give them rules to follow.

These were the Ten Commandments, written on stone tablets.

The Israelites stayed in the desert for forty years. Moses told them God's messages, with Aaron and Miriam helping him.

At last, God led the Israelites to the land he had promised them…a place flowing with milk and honey! It was called Canaan. God had kept the people safe in the desert. Now he would give them a home of their own!

Joshua

Deuteronomy 31:1–Joshua 11:23

Canaan was beautiful, but there were still dangers ahead. The people that lived there would not like the Israelites moving in! Moses prayed for a new leader to take the Israelites into the land. God chose Joshua.

"Do not be afraid," Moses told him. When Moses died, Joshua became leader. Joshua was wise and the people listened to him.

119

The time had come for the Israelites to enter Canaan. God promised Joshua that He would give them all the land they touched there. The Promised Land would stretch from river, to desert, to sea!

Joshua knew that there was a big job ahead…one that he couldn't do alone.

"Be brave," God said to Joshua. "I will be with you wherever you go."

Joshua sent two spies to check out the town of Jericho. The King soon found out, and sent soldiers to get them.

Yet a woman named Rahab hid Joshua's spies on her roof.

Rahab also sent the soldiers in the wrong direction.

When the soldiers had gone, Rahab spoke to the spies. "I know that God is going to give our land to you," she said. "But please promise that my family will be kept safe, since I helped you!" The spies agreed. Then Rahab helped them escape from the city down a long rope out of her window.

125

The spies made it safely back to the Israelite camp. They told Joshua something Rahab

had told them…that the people in Jericho were very afraid of them!

It was time to cross the Jordan River.
The priests stepped into the water.
Though the river was full, it suddenly
stopped flowing! Instead, the water
stood straight up so that the Israelites
could cross on dry land.

The people of Jericho saw the Israelites coming straight towards them. Trembling with fear, they shut all the gates to the city. No one could go in or out.

Yet God had a plan. He told Joshua to take the Israelites and march around the city once. Then they should do this on the next day, and the next. On the seventh day, they should march around seven times.

Joshua did just as God told him. The priests went first, carrying trumpets. Then came the army and the rest of the Israelites.

They marched around the city for six days. The priests blew the trumpets, but nobody was allowed to say a word.

On the seventh day,
they marched seven times.

134

The last march around, the priests blew their horns. Then Joshua yelled, "SHOUT!" The Israelites shouted, and the walls of Jericho came crumbling down!

The Israelites went into the fallen city. They found Rahab, who had helped the spies. She was unhurt! Rahab and her family were taken away to a safe place.

Then the Israelites burned the city. Everything was destroyed.

137

God helped Joshua and the
Israelites win city after city.
Soon the entire land of Canaan
was theirs! Now they could rest.

The Israelites praised God. They knew
they didn't win their battles themselves.
Instead, God was fighting for them!
He had kept His promise to give them a
beautiful land. They began to build new
homes throughout Canaan.

Deborah

Judges 4:1–5:31

The people had stopped listening to God. He punished them by handing Israel over to a cruel enemy.

The Israelites asked God to save them.

141

The leader of Israel was named Deborah. She was a very wise judge. Deborah believed that God wanted to save Israel.

Deborah called for a man named Barak, and told him to lead the army up to Mount Tabor. Then, she would trick the enemy to come to the river, where her army could attack them.

143

But the men were afraid. They said they wouldn't go unless she came with them. "Very well," said Deborah. "Then God will hand the enemy over to me."

Deborah and Barak led their army up the mountain. The enemy was coming closer! When they were very near, Deborah said "Go!" Her army rushed down the mountain…and beat the enemy!

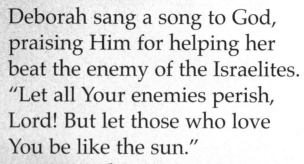

Deborah sang a song to God,
praising Him for helping her
beat the enemy of the Israelites.
"Let all Your enemies perish,
Lord! But let those who love
You be like the sun."

At last, there was peace in
Israel for many years.

Gideon

Judges 6:1–8:23

Time passed. Israel was in trouble—their enemies were closing in on them! They grew more and more afraid, as the Midianites ruined their fields and killed their animals.

The Israelites escaped to the mountains, where they lived in caves. They wondered, had God forgotten them? But He heard their prayers.

Gideon was hiding food from the
Midianites under a tree when the
Angel of the Lord came to him. "The
Lord is with you, mighty warrior,"
said the Angel.

"But sir," Gideon answered. "If the Lord is here, why are all these bad things happening to His people? Where are His miracles?"

The Angel told
Gideon that he was
being sent to save
Israel from the
Midianites. Gideon
could not believe it.
"I am the weakest
person in the weakest
clan!" he said.

Gideon placed a gift of food on a rock. Then the Angel of the Lord touched the food with fire, exploding it into flames! Now Gideon knew that the message came from God.

153

The Israelites were praying to statues, even though this was a sin. God told Gideon to tear down his father's altar. Gideon obeyed, and broke the statues in the night.

155

The enemy was getting closer. Gideon blew his horn, calling soldiers to follow him. Then he sent messengers to gather more soldiers from farther away, until he had a whole army of Israelites.

God had promised to be with Gideon. Yet Gideon still wasn't sure that he would be able to beat the Midianites.

Gideon asked God for another sign. He laid a sheepskin on the ground. Then he prayed that God would keep the ground dry but make the sheepskin wet, as a sign. The next morning, the sheepskin was wet and the ground was dry.

Then Gideon asked for a third sign. "This time, make the sheepskin dry and the ground wet." The next morning, the sheepskin was dry and the ground was wet. God had answered!

Gideon and his army camped at a spring. There were thousands and thousands of soldiers. Yet God wanted to prove that *He* was saving them. He told Gideon to bring only three hundred soldiers to fight the Midianites. Gideon chose the ones who drank with their hands.

"With only three hundred soldiers, I will help you beat the Midianites," God said. It was almost time.

161

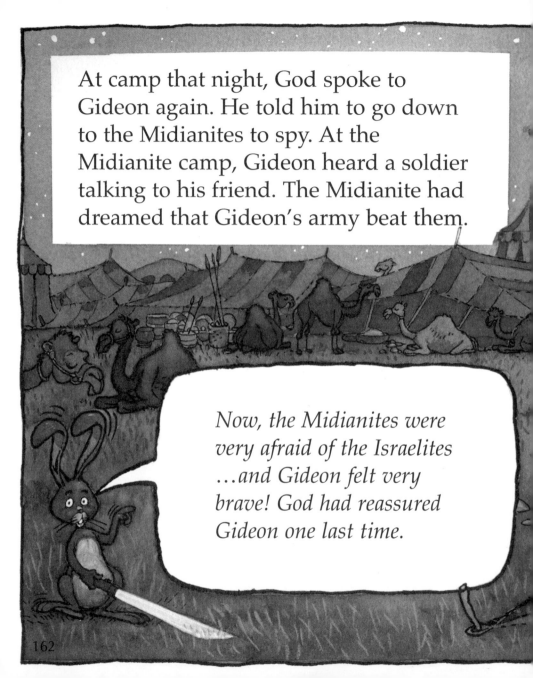

At camp that night, God spoke to Gideon again. He told him to go down to the Midianites to spy. At the Midianite camp, Gideon heard a soldier talking to his friend. The Midianite had dreamed that Gideon's army beat them.

Now, the Midianites were very afraid of the Israelites ...and Gideon felt very brave! God had reassured Gideon one last time.

Gideon hurried back to camp. "Get up!" he told his soldiers. "The Lord has given us our enemy!"

Gideon gave each soldier a torch for one hand, and a trumpet for the other. Then they marched towards the Midianites.

At the edge of the camp, the Israelites blew their horns. Then they gave a great shout. In the valley below, the Midianites became terrified and ran!

God's people had won the battle against their enemy! Gideon was thankful. He hadn't been the bravest soldier at first. But he asked God to help his faith, and God made him a mighty warrior after all!

The Israelites asked Gideon to be their king, because he had saved them from the Midianites. Gideon told them, "I will not rule over you. The Lord will!"

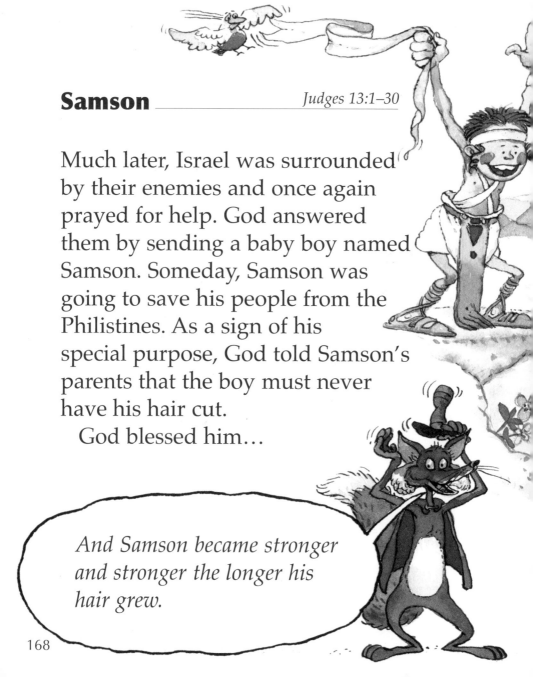

Samson

Judges 13:1–30

Much later, Israel was surrounded by their enemies and once again prayed for help. God answered them by sending a baby boy named Samson. Someday, Samson was going to save his people from the Philistines. As a sign of his special purpose, God told Samson's parents that the boy must never have his hair cut.

God blessed him…

And Samson became stronger and stronger the longer his hair grew.

One day, Samson saw
a beautiful woman.

She was from the enemy tribe,
but Samson wanted to marry
her anyway. God wanted him
to marry her, too.

Samson hurried to tell his parents that he had found the right woman for him. His parents were worried, since she was a Philistine. They didn't know that this was part of God's plan.

Samson refused to change his mind about her.

Samson and his parents made their way to the village where the woman lived.

On their way they crossed a
vineyard. All of a sudden, a huge
lion came out of nowhere!

The lion pounced, but it was no match for Samson. God was with him. Samson killed the lion with his bare hands!

When the day came for Samson to go and get his new wife, he saw the dead lion on the side of the road. A swarm of bees had made a hive inside. Samson ate some of the honey.

Samson made up a riddle about the beehive in the lion: "Out of the eater came something to eat. Out of the strong came something sweet." When he arrived at the village, he asked the Philistines if they could guess the answer to the riddle.

They couldn't guess the riddle, so they tricked Samson's wife into telling them.

Samson was angry about their trick. But then, the Philistines made him angrier by taking his wife away from him. So Samson caught three hundred foxes, put their tails on fire, and let them go in the Philistines' fields.

All their grain burned!

181

His enemies came to arrest Samson, tying him with rope. The Philistines shouted at him—finally they had caught the mighty Samson! Then suddenly, the Spirit of the Lord filled Samson. He became so strong that he snapped the ropes right off!

He was a mighty warrior. The Israelites made Samson ruler.

One day, Samson fell in love with a woman named Delilah. The Philistines thought, "This is our chance!" They went to Delilah, and promised her silver if she could find out the secret of Samson's strength.

Delilah begged Samson to tell her his secret. At first he refused, but finally he got so tired of her asking that he gave in. He told her that if his hair were cut, he would become weak.

The Philistines came and cut his hair while he was asleep.

Samson became as weak as any other man. The Philistines hurt his eyes so he couldn't see, then threw him in jail. They rejoiced, thanking their god for giving them their enemy. Though little did they know, Samson was getting stronger as his hair began to grow again!

While the Philistines were celebrating inside the temple, they had Samson brought out from jail so that they could laugh at him. Samson stood between two pillars. Then he called out to God—"Lord, make me strong just once more!" Samson put his hands against the pillars. "Let me die with the Philistines!"

With one mighty push, the temple came toppling down. All of the Philistine leaders were killed! Samson had given up his own life, too, but he was a mighty hero because he had fulfilled God's purpose for him by saving Israel.

189

A long time passed. There was a famine in the land, so Naomi's family moved to Moab where her sons got married. One day, her husband died. Then her sons died, too. Sad Naomi decided to return home to Israel.

Naomi told her son's wife, Ruth, to go home to her own mother.

But Ruth refused to leave her mother-in-law. "Where you go I will go. Your people will be my people, and your God will be my God," said Ruth.

Naomi finally agreed to let Ruth go to Israel with her. They set out on the long journey together. At last, they arrived at Naomi's home town, Bethlehem.

The people of Bethlehem said, "Is this Naomi?" Naomi told them that her husband and sons had died. She was heartbroken. Yet Ruth stayed right by her side, taking care of her.

Naomi and Ruth needed food. Ruth went to the fields and picked up the leftover grain from the harvest.

Boaz owned the field. "Who is that?" he asked when he saw Ruth. "That's Naomi's daughter-in-law," his servants said. Boaz saw that Ruth was helping Naomi, so he was kind to her.

197

Boaz was Naomi's relative. He loved and cared about Naomi and Ruth.

Naomi hoped Boaz would help Ruth find a new husband. She told Ruth to go and sleep at his feet. Then they would hear what Boaz said.

The next day, Ruth told Naomi what had happened. Boaz had been surprised when he saw her. He knew that she was good, so he promised to do anything she asked.

Ruth wished to marry. Boaz had sent her away with grain, promising that tomorrow she would have a new husband.

Ruth and Boaz were soon married!
Boaz was happy to be loved by Ruth.
Ruth was happy to be loved by Boaz.
They were both faithful to God,
so God was faithful to them!

God chose them for each other. Their marriage was part of His perfect plan for their lives.

The elders blessed Ruth and Boaz.
"May you have many children!"
they said.

Everyone knew how lucky Naomi was to have a daughter-in-law like Ruth, who loved her so much. Now Naomi might have grandchildren, after all!

Sure enough, Ruth gave birth to a son. He was named Obed. Boaz and Ruth loved Obed very much. So did Naomi. Naomi cared for him as if he were her own.

Ruth rejoiced. She was once sad, but God did not forget her! He gave her a new family because she was faithful and kind.

207

David

Years passed. Israel decided that they wanted a king, and Saul became ruler. But Saul sinned, so God chose someone new to lead Israel.

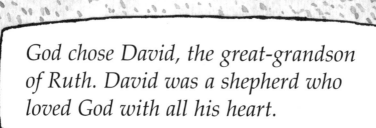

God chose David, the great-grandson of Ruth. David was a shepherd who loved God with all his heart.

209

David took good care of his father's sheep.

211

One day God told His prophet Samuel to go and anoint the new king, a son of Jesse in Bethlehem. Samuel looked at each of Jesse's big strong sons. God reminded Samuel that the Lord does not look at appearances, but at the heart. Samuel said to Jesse, "God has not chosen him, or him, or him."

"Only David, the smallest," Jesse answered. "He is tending the sheep." Samuel had him brought in. When Samuel saw David, God showed him that this was the one. He had chosen a boy as the next king! Samuel took the oil and anointed him, and the Spirit of the Lord filled David.

From that day on, David was powerful in all he did.

Israel was at war with the
Philistines. The Israelites had
one major problem—the enemy
had a giant, named Goliath, on
their side!

217

Goliath shouted, "Send someone to fight me!" David's brothers and the other soldiers were too afraid. But just then, David came along to bring his brothers food and heard the giant. David went to King Saul. "I will fight Goliath!" he said.

"God will help me," David promised Saul.

219

Saul gave David his own armour to wear. It was too big for him, so David left it behind with the weapons. He collected five smooth stones instead, and put them in his pouch. Then David went right up to Goliath.

"You come with a sword, but I come in the name of the Lord!" he shouted. "The battle is the Lord's, and today He will save Israel so that the whole world will know He is God!"

Goliath saw that David was only a boy. The giant was not afraid, and moved closer to attack David. With his slingshot in one hand, David pulled out a stone.

David swung his slingshot. The stone flew, hitting Goliath right in the head! The giant fell face down onto the ground.

223

David had killed the giant!
He stood over him and cut
off the enormous head.

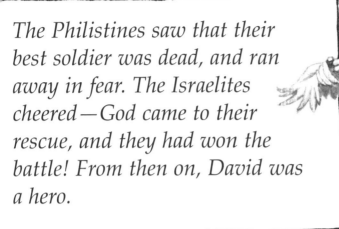

The Philistines saw that their best soldier was dead, and ran away in fear. The Israelites cheered—God came to their rescue, and they had won the battle! From then on, David was a hero.

David led many more battles just as bravely. God was with him everywhere he went. King Saul became jealous because the people liked David better than him, so he tried to kill him. But God kept David safe.

After Saul had died, David was crowned King, just as God had planned.

David was a good and powerful king because he obeyed God even when it was difficult.

228

David had many enemies against him. Yet no matter how many bad things happened, David always trusted in the Lord. God never failed to rescue him from danger, rewarding his faith with a long reign as king. And David never failed to sing his praise of thankfulness to God!

Solomon

1 Kings 2:1–10:13; Proverbs

David grew old, and it was time to find a new king for Israel. David chose his son Solomon. David said to him, "Be strong, and follow God!" When David died, Solomon became ruler.

Solomon had a dream when he was a young king. In the dream, God said, "Ask for anything you want."

Solomon answered, "Lord, give me a wise heart so that I will know right from wrong."

God was happy with Solomon's wish. Because he had asked for wisdom instead of riches, God promised him both wisdom and *riches!*

People came from all around to ask for Solomon's advice. One day, two women came to see him. They were fighting over a baby. "He's my son!" shouted one woman.

"No! He's mine!" said the other. It seemed impossible to know who the real mother was…

...but wise Solomon had a plan to find out.

"Cut the baby in half," said Solomon. "Then they can share him."

The real mother quickly cried out, "Give her the baby, but don't hurt him!"

Now Solomon knew who had told the truth. "Give the baby to the first woman," he said. He knew that she was the real mother, because she refused to see the baby hurt. Only a mother would care more about the baby's life than her own selfish wishes.

The people of Israel heard the story, and realized how bright Solomon was. He knew how to rule fairly. He also taught about plants and animals, birds and fish. Soon, people came from other countries with expensive gifts for Solomon. Everyone wanted to listen to the wisest man on earth.

God had given Solomon understanding as wide as the sea.

Solomon ruled all the way from the Euphrates River to Egypt. Because of his wisdom, he gained great armies and great wealth.

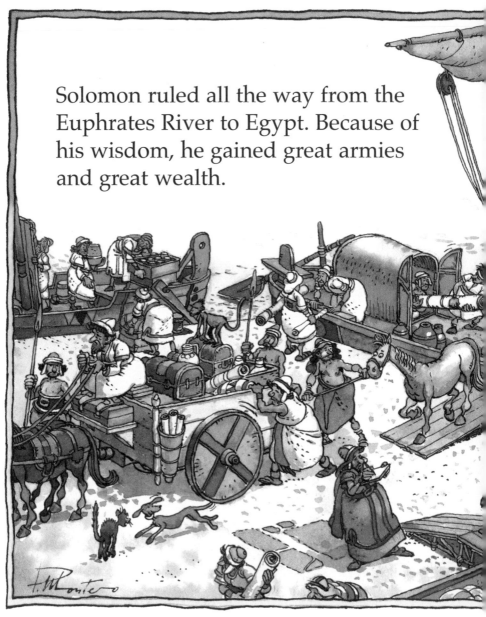

While David had been king, there was war after war. Now, it was peaceful. Since there was plenty of food as well, the people were content and happy.

Solomon wanted to build a house for God.

With stone and wood, he built a glorious temple. Then he covered the inside with gold from floor to ceiling!

243

The Queen of Sheba heard about Solomon, and came to ask him her hardest questions. Yet nothing was too difficult for Solomon to explain.

Solomon taught many lessons to help people live good lives. He said that a good man works hard and is happy with what he has.

But a rich man won't be happy if he always wants more.

A woman that loves God is strong, and speaks with wisdom. People call her blessed.

Solomon said that children should listen to their mother and father, because their parents' words are like a light to guide them. Parents should love their children by teaching them right from wrong. They should also discipline them to give them hope for a good future.

Solomon had everything he could wish for. His palace was filled with gold. He had a very large family, and was famous near and far. Yet most importantly, he had the wisdom to love God.

When Solomon was much older, he disobeyed the Lord by worshipping other gods. Though God was very angry about this, He had promised David not to punish Solomon.

Solomon died, but his wise words live on forever. They remind people everywhere that the greatest wealth is to know God. After all, everything else comes from Him!

Elijah

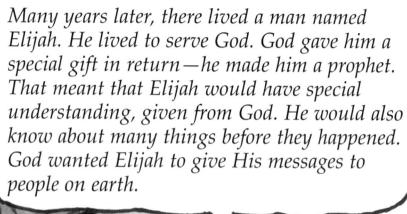

Many years later, there lived a man named Elijah. He lived to serve God. God gave him a special gift in return—he made him a prophet. That meant that Elijah would have special understanding, given from God. He would also know about many things before they happened. God wanted Elijah to give His messages to people on earth.

King Ahab sinned by building
a statue and worshipping it.
This made God unhappy.

Elijah gave the King a message from God. "There will be no more rain until I say," Elijah told him. The King became angry, but God gave Elijah a hiding place to stay safe. The Lord would protect him and take care of him during the drought.

Elijah went to the brook that God had told him about, near the Jordan River. He stayed there day after day.

God kept His promise to provide for Elijah—He sent ravens to feed him! Every morning and every night, they brought Elijah bread and meat. He drank water from the brook.

After a while, the brook dried up. God spoke to Elijah again, and told him to go to a town called Zarephath. "I have commanded a widow there to provide for you," God said.

257

Elijah found the woman God had told him about. He asked her for bread, but she had only a tiny bit of flour and oil. Elijah promised that if she fed him, she and her son would have plenty to eat. Sure enough, her flour and oil never ran out!

One day, the woman's son died. Elijah prayed. Then God brought the boy back to life!

After three years, Elijah went back to see King Ahab. The King blamed Elijah for the drought, but Elijah told the King that he had caused the drought himself by serving other gods. God was angry at Israel for bowing to statues.

Then Elijah told the King to gather all the prophets of different gods and meet him on top of Mount Carmel.

They were going to have a contest to see whose was the true God!

261

Elijah said that they would each build an altar, and call on their own god. The false prophets prayed and prayed, but all was still.

Elijah poured water on his altar. Then he called out to God. Suddenly, his altar burst into flames! The others fell to the ground, saying "The Lord is God!"

Soon a small cloud began to rise over the sea. Elijah sent his servant to tell King Ahab to hurry down the mountain. Rain was coming, at last!

The sky grew black and stormy.
The King got in his chariot and hurried
towards the town of Jezreel. Suddenly
God filled Elijah with strength, and on
his own feet he beat King Ahab to the
city gates!

When the King told Queen Jezebel what Elijah had done on the mountaintop, she was angry. Elijah escaped into the wilderness.

One night, while he was sleeping in a cave, the Lord told him to go outside. God wanted to show himself to Elijah.

A storm came. Then an earthquake. Then a fire. But God was not in any of these things. Instead, He was in the small breeze that came last.

God told Elijah to anoint a new king. Afterwards, Elijah anointed Elisha as the next prophet.

Elijah delivered God's messages, though the people didn't always like them. Twice, a king sent fifty soldiers to capture Elijah.

Elijah called on God, and fire came down from heaven to protect him.

269

It was almost time for Elijah to go and be with God in heaven. But first, he visited many cities. Elijah told Elisha to stay behind, but Elisha refused to leave his side. When they came to the Jordan River, Elijah prayed and the water was divided so they could cross. Then Elijah said to Elisha, "What can I give you?" Elisha asked for a spirit like Elijah's.

Suddenly, a chariot of fire appeared! Elijah was taken up to heaven in a whirlwind.

When Elisha crossed the river alone, he was able to split the water like Elijah had. His wish was granted!

Esther

Esther and Mordecai were cousins. Long ago, their great grandfather had been stolen away from Israel. That made Esther and Mordecai Jews, though they lived in Persia.

One day, the King of Persia decided to find a new queen. He gathered the most beautiful women from all around. Esther was one of those chosen to go to the royal palace.

But before she went, Mordecai warned her not to tell anyone that she was Jewish.

Esther and the other women stayed in the palace for one year. They ate the best food and were given beautiful clothes and jewelry to wear. The servants pampered them with oils and perfume. All the while, Mordecai stayed nearby the palace.

Everyone liked Esther because she was so beautiful and good.

When the King met her, it didn't take him long to choose a wife. Esther was his favourite! The king put the royal crown on her head to make Esther queen.

Then he held a great feast for her. He declared a holiday throughout the land, giving expensive gifts. The King loved and trusted Esther very much.

Haman was an important leader. He wanted everyone to bow to him, but Mordecai refused. Mordecai was Jewish and only bowed to God. This made Haman so angry that he created a plan to kill all the Jews in the land.

Haman told the King, "The Jews don't follow our laws, so lets destroy them!" Since the King listened to Haman's advice, he agreed that all the Jews would be killed on a certain day. When the Jews heard the news, they put on sackcloth and cried out to God.

279

280

"Speak to the King for us!" the message said. "Maybe this is the reason God made you queen."

Esther agreed to the plan. She sent a message back to Mordecai, telling him to pray with the Jews for three days. Then Esther went to see the King.

Esther was very brave. After all, what would the King do when he found out that she was Jewish? He might kill her for not telling him earlier!

The King was happy to see Esther.
He held out his golden sceptre, to
show that she was allowed to speak.
"What do you wish, Queen Esther?"
the King said.

"Would the King and Haman
please come to the banquet I've
made for them?" she asked.

At the dinner, Esther said to the King, "My wish is that you save me and my people, because someone is trying to kill us!"

The King answered, "Who would dare do such a thing?"

Esther pointed to Haman. Terrified, Haman begged Esther for his life. But it was too late—the King ordered Haman to be hanged!

Esther told the King that Mordecai was her cousin. The King gave Mordecai his ring, and put him in Haman's place. Then Esther begged the King to change the order to kill the Jews. The King happily agreed. The Jews would be protected and honoured, instead.

When the Jews heard this, they celebrated with joy. God had used brave Esther to save her people!

Daniel

Daniel 1:1–6:27

There was a terrible war in Israel.
The King of Babylon attacked Jerusalem,
stealing the treasure from their temples.
He also took many Israelites and
brought them to his own land.

One of the prisoners was a boy named Daniel. Daniel followed God with his whole heart. He was wise and brave, keeping his eyes on what was right.

When they had reached Babylon, the King ordered a servant to gather the strongest and brightest of the Israelite boys. They were going to get special teaching.

The boys would study the language and stories of their new home. After three years of school, they would be ready to serve the King.

The King gave them fine food and wine.

But Daniel did not want to eat like the Babylonians. He reminded his friends that they were from Israel, and had their own ways of doing things. Most importantly, they must follow God and pray only to him.

Daniel asked his teacher to let the Jewish
boys eat only vegetables and drink only
water. "But you will get thin and weak!"
answered his teacher. "Then the King will
have me killed."

Daniel asked his teacher to test his wish
to see what would happen. The teacher
liked Daniel, so he agreed. For ten days,
Daniel and his friends had only vegetables
and water.

At the end of the test, the teacher saw that the Jewish boys had grown stronger than the others. He then allowed them to follow God's rules for them.

Daniel and his friends became so smart that the King heard about it and brought them to do important work for him. Daniel, though, was not only smart—he could also understand signs from God.

One day, the King gave a party.
His guests were feasting and
worshipping statues…

…*when suddenly,
a hand appeared
and began writing
on the wall!
The King grew
pale. He was very
afraid!*

God filled Daniel with understanding. "God is angry with you for stealing and worshipping other gods," Daniel told the King. Then the King made Daniel an important leader.

The other leaders became jealous, and planned a trick. They got the King to order everyone to bow to him. But Daniel would only bow to God. "Throw him in the lions' den!" said his enemies.

303

Though the King loved Daniel, he was forced to punish him. And so, Daniel was thrown down into the den of lions. Then he trusted in God with all his might.

God answered Daniel's faith! He sent an angel to shut the lions' mouths.

The next morning, the King rushed to the den to see what had happened. He cried into the opening, "Daniel, has your God been able to save you from the lions?"

Daniel called back that he was safe, and was then pulled out of the den without a scratch. The King happily declared, "To everyone on earth—the one Daniel worships is the true God forever, who rescues and makes miracles!"

Jonah

Jonah 1:1–4:11

In a town called Nineveh,
the people were doing
bad things. God loved
them still. He chose a
man named Jonah to go
to the town and tell them
to stop sinning.

Jonah didn't want to go to Nineveh, because the people there were his enemies.

Jonah decided not to obey God. He ran away instead, on a boat headed for Spain.

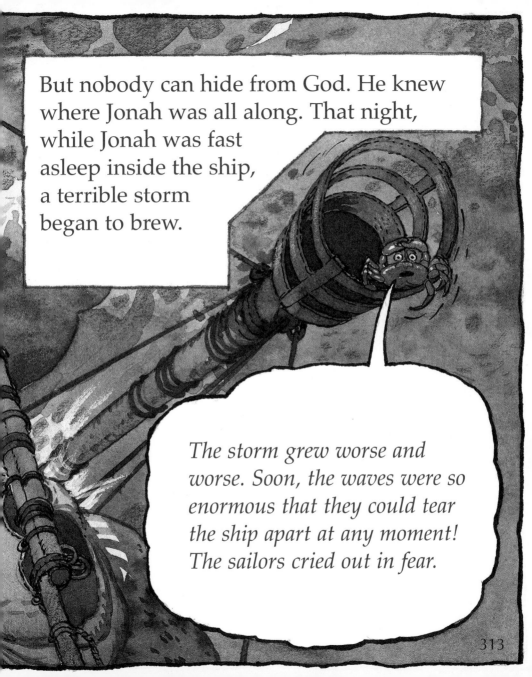

But nobody can hide from God. He knew where Jonah was all along. That night, while Jonah was fast asleep inside the ship, a terrible storm began to brew.

The storm grew worse and worse. Soon, the waves were so enormous that they could tear the ship apart at any moment! The sailors cried out in fear.

313

Yet Jonah was the most afraid of all, because he knew why the storm had come…God was angry with him!

"Throw me overboard!" said Jonah. "Then the storm will stop."

With one big splash, Jonah landed in the sea. Though the storm grew calm, it seemed Jonah was suddenly in more trouble than ever! But just as God had been with Jonah while he was trying to hide, God was with him now…

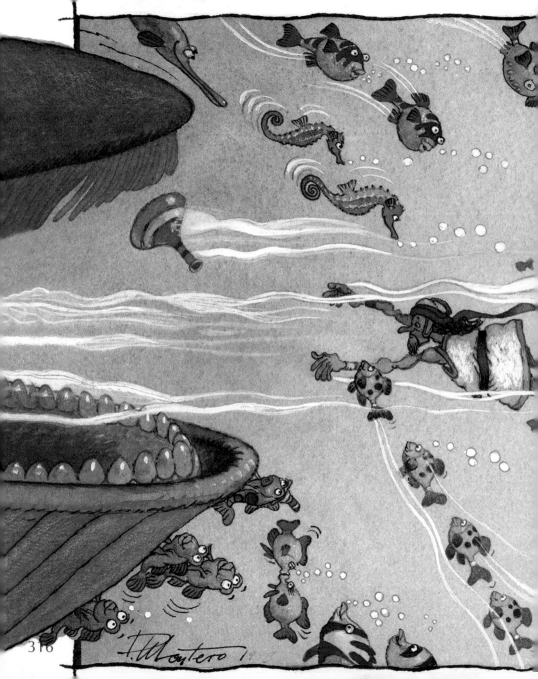

God sent a giant fish to swallow
Jonah up! It was dark and strange
inside the fish, but Jonah prayed
and prayed. He told God how
sorry he was for trying to run
away.

317

Jonah had finally learned his lesson.
So at last, God told the fish to
spit Jonah onto a beach. Jonah was
grateful to be on land.

This time, Jonah obeyed. When he got to Nineveh, he went through the streets telling everyone that God would soon destroy the town because they were sinning.

The people listened to Jonah, realizing that the message was from God.

The people in Nineveh wanted to show God how sorry they were, so they took off their nice clothes and put on sacks instead. The whole town prayed to God, begging His forgiveness for having done wrong.

And sure enough, it wasn't too late—

God heard their prayers and forgave them!

323

When God didn't destroy the city after all, Jonah became upset. "I knew you would forgive them. That's why I didn't want to come!" He left Nineveh and sat down by himself. Yet even in Jonah's anger, God did not leave him.

God made a plant sprout right where Jonah sat. It grew and grew, and Jonah enjoyed its shade.

The next morning, God sent along a worm to chew the plant so that the leaves died. Now Jonah was really angry! He no longer had any shelter. When the wind blew, he shivered. When the sun shone, he got burned. Jonah thought he would rather die. And still, he was not alone.

God had a lesson for him. "You cared about this plant, even though it only lived for one day. So shouldn't I care about the thousands of people in Nineveh?" God cared so much that He saved the city through one man!

Mary

Luke 1:26–2:20

A long time passed. God looked at the world, and decided it was time to send His most precious gift of all—His own Son! God sent an angel to a girl named Mary.

329

Mary answered the angel, "I am the Lord's servant. May His will be done."

Then Mary hurried to a town in the hill country of Judea. She went to the house of her cousin Elizabeth, who was also pregnant. When she heard Mary coming, Elizabeth was filled with the Holy Spirit. "Blessed are you!" Elizabeth exclaimed. "You are carrying the Son of God."

Mary sang a song to God, praising
Him for His miracle.

"My spirit rejoices in the Lord!
He has seen me
And done great things for me—
Holy is His name!
He is good to those who love Him
Through all times
He does the impossible
He destroys evil
And feeds the hungry.
He has helped Israel
Remembering His promises
To those that came before us!"

Mary was engaged to a man named Joseph. Soon Joseph learned that Mary was going to have a baby. He didn't understand why she was pregnant before they were married.

But then an angel came to him in a dream. "Don't be afraid—the baby inside Mary comes from God. You shall call him Jesus."

The ruler gave an order that everyone had to get registered. Joseph and Mary went on a long journey to Bethlehem, where Joseph was from.

Mary rode on a donkey all the way from their home in Nazareth. The baby in her belly had grown very large.

338

When they finally got to Bethlehem, there was no room for them. All the inns were full. Finally they found a stable…

…where at least it was warm and dry. Joseph and Mary stayed there with the animals.

It was time for Jesus to be born! Mary
wrapped Him lovingly in clothes, while
the animals looked on.

The angels in heaven rejoiced. God's Son had arrived!

Nearby, shepherds were watching their sheep. An angel appeared to them, saying, "I bring you tidings of great joy—Christ is born!" They hurried to see Jesus.

They followed a giant star to find Him.
After many months, they arrived.

They brought expensive gifts of gold,
frankincense, and myrrh. Then they
worshipped Jesus.

Mary loved her son Jesus. Joseph loved Him too, and took care of Him like he was His real father.

Because Mary was faithful, God had given her a very special job. All over the world, she would always be remembered as the mother of God's Son!

347

Jesus' parents took Him to the temple. A godly man named Simeon blessed baby Jesus, saying, "You are the light who will save all people!"

Anna was a prophetess who lived in the temple. When she saw Jesus, she too realized that He was the Lord.

349

One night Joseph had a dream. God told him, "Jesus is in danger. Run away to Egypt!"

King Herod had heard that a new king was born. He was jealous, and wanted to kill baby Jesus. But God had warned Joseph and Mary through the dream. They obeyed God and went to Egypt, where they lived safely.

When God told them it was safe, Joseph and Mary took Jesus home to Nazareth. The Child grew. He became strong and wise, because God smiled on Him.

Jesus and His family went to Jerusalem for a feast. When it was over, Joseph and Mary left for home. But before long they realized that Jesus was missing!

They went back to Jerusalem to look for Him. Finally, they found Him in the temple— teaching the teachers about God!

"We have been worried about you," said His mother.

"Didn't you know I would be in the temple, doing God's work?" Jesus replied. His parents did not understand what He meant, but they were happy He was safe.

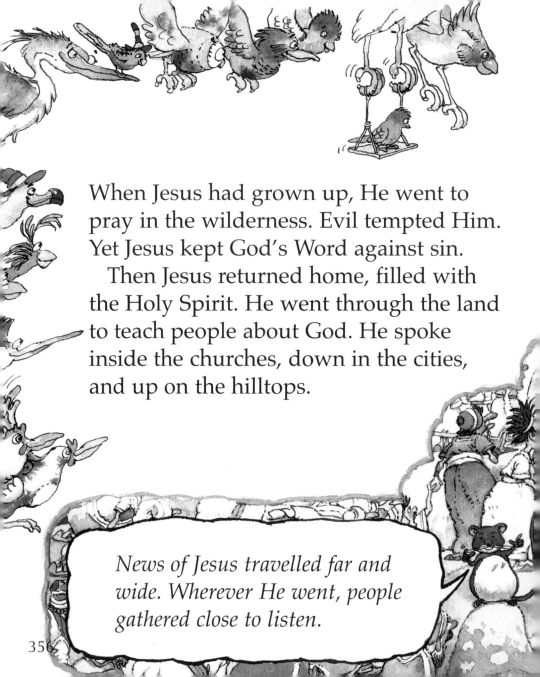

When Jesus had grown up, He went to pray in the wilderness. Evil tempted Him. Yet Jesus kept God's Word against sin.

Then Jesus returned home, filled with the Holy Spirit. He went through the land to teach people about God. He spoke inside the churches, down in the cities, and up on the hilltops.

News of Jesus travelled far and wide. Wherever He went, people gathered close to listen.

Jesus performed miracles, as well. People with all kinds of sicknesses came to Him, and He healed them!

One day, Jesus was teaching in a house among important leaders. There was a crippled man outside who wanted to see Jesus, but the house was full. So the man's friends cut a hole in the roof, and lowered him down. Jesus saw that the man and his friends had faith. He said to the crippled man, "Get up!" The man obeyed. He could walk!

Jesus said, "Blessed are those who suffer, because they will be rewarded in heaven." He taught that we should be kind to our enemies, because God loves them. Jesus said that if we give, then we will be given to.

If we plant goodness in our hearts, good things will grow from us.

One day, Jesus and His disciples were crossing a lake. Jesus fell asleep.

Suddenly, a storm arose! The boat
began to fill with water. The disciples
woke Jesus up, crying, "We are going
to drown!"

Jesus commanded the storm to stop. All was calm. Then He said to His disciples, "Where is your faith?"

The disciples were amazed—the wind and waves obeyed Jesus!

Jesus was teaching a huge crowd when it began to get late. There was nothing for them to eat. Then a boy gave Jesus his own supper—two fish and five loaves of bread. Jesus blessed the food. Then He began to break it…and filled basket after basket! All five thousand people ate until they were full.

367

Jesus told a story to explain what it means to love your neighbour.

A man was robbed and left on the side of the road. A priest walked by, and pretended not to notice.
A second person passed and didn't help either.

Then a man from a different country came along. He felt sorry when he saw the hurt man, and stopped to help him. He bandaged his wounds. Then the Samaritan carried the hurt man to an inn, and paid the innkeeper to care for him.

Jesus was on His way to Jerusalem when He came to a village. "Jesus, help us!" He heard people crying out. The voices came from ten sick men. Jesus said to them, "Go and see the priests!"

As the men walked away, Jesus performed a miracle—they were all healed! The men were overjoyed. Yet only one of them returned to thank Jesus. He fell down at Jesus' feet, praising Him. Jesus said to him, "You are well because you believed."

The children wanted to see Jesus too. The disciples tried to send them away, but Jesus said, "Let the little children come to Me!" Then He blessed the children.

"You must each become like a child in order to enter the kingdom of God," Jesus told the disciples.

Jesus loved children very much. He said that they are special because they don't worry about being important. And sometimes, children even understand things that adults cannot. Jesus said, "Whoever welcomes a child welcomes Me."

A blind man sat begging when Jesus came near Jericho. The blind man wanted to know why the people were passing by. When he heard that Jesus was near, he cried out, "Jesus, have mercy on me!" The people tried to quiet him, but he just called out louder.

Jesus heard him and stopped. "I want to see!" said the man. Jesus healed his eyes. The man leaped with joy! The people who saw the miracle praised the Lord, too.

Jesus healed many sick, and even raised people from the dead. But most importantly, He forgave their sins. Many people did not understand why He forgave people who were bad. But Jesus said that God rejoices for every person that turns away from sin. Each is precious to the Lord!

375

Peter  _Matthew 4:18–26:75_

Jesus had been walking by the Sea of Galilee. He saw two brothers named Simon and Andrew, throwing their nets into the sea. They were fishermen.

Jesus said to them, "Follow Me. I will make you fishers of men." Simon and Andrew left their nets and followed Jesus. As they walked along the sea, Jesus called to James and John, who were in a boat. They also followed Jesus. Jesus chose twelve men in all.

Simon and the other disciples
followed Jesus from place to
place, listening and learning.

379

One day, Jesus sent His disciples ahead in a boat while He went to pray. Soon a storm grew, tossing the boat. The disciples looked up, and whom should they see but Jesus—walking on the water towards them! At first He looked like a ghost.

Simon cried out, "If it's really you Lord, let me walk to You on the water!" Jesus told him to come. Simon stepped onto the water. Then he realized how strong the wind was, and became afraid. Suddenly Simon began to sink! Jesus reached out and caught him. "Why did you doubt?" He said. Then they got into the boat, and the storm grew still.

One day Jesus asked His disciples,
"Who do people say that I am?"
Simon answered, "You are the Christ,
Son of God."

Jesus told His disciples that He must soon go to Jerusalem to be killed. Yet on the third day, He would rise again. Peter said, "Surely this won't happen to *You*, Lord!"

Jesus turned to Peter. "You don't understand the ways of God," He said.

Jesus and His disciples came near Jerusalem. They found a donkey for Jesus. Large crowds had gathered to welcome Him, spreading clothes on the ground for Him to ride on. They waved branches and cried out, "Hosanna! Blessed is He!"

386

Jesus said to them, "One of you will sell Me to the enemy." The disciples were sad…but Judas knew that Jesus was speaking about him.

Jesus blessed the bread and wine, and gave some to each disciple. He told them to remember Him when they ate from now on.

Jesus took His disciples to a garden. He was very sad, falling on the ground to speak to God. "Your will be done," Jesus prayed.

Suddenly men appeared, with clubs and swords! Judas had brought the leaders with soldiers, to take Jesus away. Peter drew his sword, and cut off the ear of one of the men.

Jesus told Peter to put his sword away, then healed the man's ear. "I must go," Jesus said. "This is God's plan."

The disciples became afraid and ran away. Jesus' enemies took Him to be judged.

When the people saw Peter, they said to him, "You were with Jesus!" But Peter replied, "No I wasn't—I don't even know Him." Three times, Peter lied about knowing Jesus. Then a cockerel crowed. Peter realized that he had betrayed Jesus.

Peter wept, very sorry for what he had done.

391

Mary & Martha

Jesus stood before the people. The judge asked the crowd what should be done to Jesus.
"Kill Him on the cross!" they yelled.

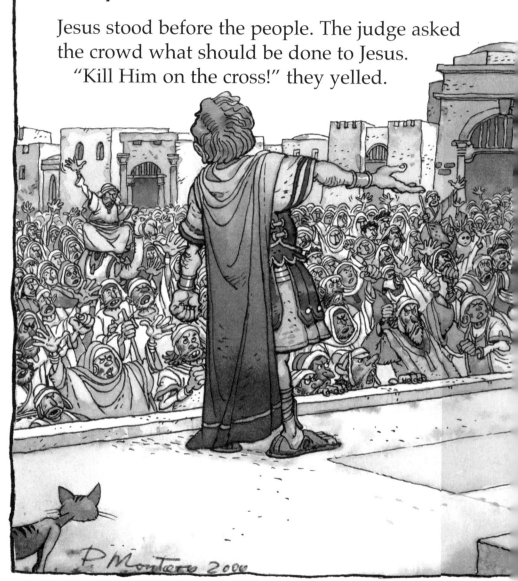

The soldiers hurt Jesus, then hung Him on the cross. Mary, Martha, and Jesus' mother Mary loved Jesus. They stood nearby, weeping.

395

396

Over Jesus' head, the soldiers hung a sign that said, "This is Jesus, the King of the Jews." His enemies made fun of Him. "If You are really the Son of God, then make a miracle by getting down from the cross!"

Jesus cried out to God. Then His spirit left His body.

After Jesus had died, His friends took His body off the cross. They wrapped Him in clean clothes. Then they laid Him in a tomb of rock. Mary and Martha were terribly sad. Their beloved Jesus was gone.

After three days had passed, the women went to see the tomb. Suddenly, there was a great earthquake! An angel from heaven rolled the stone away from the tomb's opening. Then he sat on top of the stone, shining like lightening! The guards shook with fear.

Then the angel spoke to Jesus' friends. "Don't be afraid. I know you are looking for Jesus. He isn't here—He is risen!" The women could hardly believe their ears.

"Come and see for yourselves," the angel said to them. Mary, Martha, and Jesus' mother went into the tomb. Sure enough, Jesus was gone! All that remained in the place He had been were the cloths He was wrapped in.

"Go and tell His disciples that Jesus is risen from the dead," the angel said. "You will see Jesus on the road." The women were overjoyed, and ran to tell the disciples.

Jesus met them along the way, as the angel promised. "Rejoice!" He said. They worshipped Jesus, then hurried on.

401

The disciples were gathered together, weeping and mourning Jesus' death. All of a sudden, Mary burst through the door. She told the men that she had seen the Lord—alive! The disciples were amazed...how could it be true? John and Peter raced to the tomb.

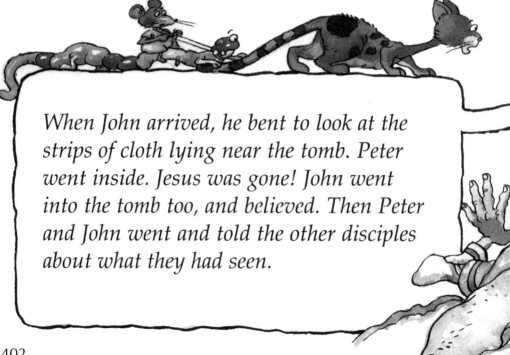

When John arrived, he bent to look at the strips of cloth lying near the tomb. Peter went inside. Jesus was gone! John went into the tomb too, and believed. Then Peter and John went and told the other disciples about what they had seen.

One evening, the disciples were gathered together indoors. They were hiding from those that wanted to hurt them for having been friends with Jesus. To their sudden amazement, Jesus appeared! "Peace be with you," He said.

The disciples were overjoyed to see Him. Jesus showed them His wounds. Then He gave them a special message— He was sending them into the world to do His work!

Jesus gave the disciples the Holy Spirit. It would help them in the days to come.

It was time for Jesus to return to heaven, so He led the disciples out of the city. There He told them, "Go and teach people everywhere that Jesus came to forgive their sins."

He lifted His hands and blessed them. Then He was taken to heaven, right before their eyes! They were amazed. As He disappeared in a cloud, the disciples worshipped.

The disciples returned to Jerusalem. There they joined Mary and Martha to pray. As they were filled with the Holy Spirit, they spoke in new languages. Then the disciples went out to preach God's Word as Jesus had taught them.

Paul

Acts 7:54–1 Corinthians 13:7

Not everyone was happy to hear about Jesus. Stephen was taken to be killed for sharing about Him.

411

Saul wanted to destroy the church. One day, he was on his way to Damascus to look for believers. He was going to bring them back to Jerusalem as prisoners.

Suddenly, a light from heaven flashed around him!

Saul fell to the ground. "Saul, why do you hurt Me?" he heard a voice say.

"Who are you?" Saul asked.

"I am Jesus, who you are fighting against," the voice replied. "Get up and go into the city, and I will tell you what you must do." The men travelling with Saul heard the voice too, and were stunned. When Saul got up from the ground, his eyes were open but he couldn't see. His men had to lead him by the hand into the city. When he got to Damascus, he prayed and prayed.

For three days, Saul was blind. Then the Lord filled him with the Holy Spirit, and he could see again! Saul went to be baptized. From then on, he was called Paul instead of Saul.

Paul spent several days in Damascus, preaching that Jesus had come as the Son of God. The people were amazed, wondering, "Isn't this Saul, who came to arrest those that believe in Jesus?"

Paul went to Jerusalem. He wanted to join the disciples, but they were afraid of him because of the bad things he had done before. Then the disciple Barnabas told the others how Saul had met the Lord, and how he had preached in Damascus.

Then the disciples let him stay with them. Together, they taught about Jesus. More and more people listened and believed.

Paul and his friends travelled far to spread the good news. One day, Paul and Silas were thrown in jail for preaching. Yet their chains didn't stop them from singing praises to God.

Suddenly, the prison doors flew open! The prison guard trembled, asking, "What must I do to be saved?" Paul and Silas answered that he must believe in Jesus. The guard was grateful.

Then Paul and Silas were released.

Paul got arrested again, and was being sent to Rome. As the ship sailed along, the waters grew rough. After awhile the wind was so strong that they gave up trying to steer the ship. The people believed they would die. They wanted to try and escape in the lifeboats.

But Paul told them, "Be brave! Last night, an angel told me that you will all live if you stay on the ship." They listened to Paul and stayed on board.

That night, Paul gave thanks to God. Then he ordered everyone to eat. When the morning came, they saw an island! They ran the ship onto the sand, and everyone swam safely to shore.

The islanders were kind to the strangers, building a fire for them. Then the leader of the island welcomed them into his home. The leader's father was sick, but Paul healed him.

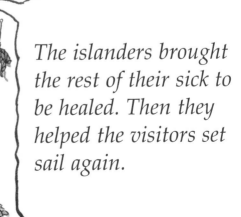

The islanders brought the rest of their sick to be healed. Then they helped the visitors set sail again.

Paul was still a prisoner when
they arrived in Rome, with a soldier
to guard him. Yet he was free to go
where he wanted and teach. The people
there wanted to hear about God and
His Son Jesus.

Paul said that if they would open their hearts, God would heal them.

The more Paul preached, the more his enemies tried to hurt him. Paul was very brave by answering when questioned. He was thrown in jail again and again.

In jail, Paul wrote about how to live by God's Word. He said that the Holy Spirit would teach us wisdom if we asked. He said that faith is nothing, unless we have love. Love is patient and kind, not envious or rude.

Love rejoices in the truth. It always protects, always trusts, and always hopes.

Paul had once been an enemy to Jesus, but God changed his heart. He wanted to use Paul to spread His Word. Paul chose to obey God's special call, travelling all over to tell the world that Jesus had come to earth to forgive them.

John

Acts 5:12–5:24; 1 John–Revelation

John was one of the twelve disciples. He had watched Jesus perform miracles, and listened closely to His teachings.

John loved Jesus, and Jesus loved John.
Jesus wanted John close when He was sad.

433

After Jesus left earth, John and the disciples spread His teachings. Many people were saved. Some of the leaders were bothered by the miracles and teachings of John and Peter. They threw them in jail over and over to try to stop them. Yet the disciples refused to quit. Behind bars, they wrote letters to lead Jesus' followers.

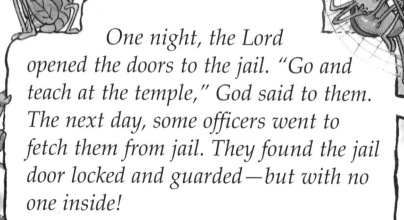

One night, the Lord opened the doors to the jail. "Go and teach at the temple," God said to them. The next day, some officers went to fetch them from jail. They found the jail door locked and guarded—but with no one inside!

In his letters, John said that God is light and not darkness. We can't know God if we live in the darkness of sin.

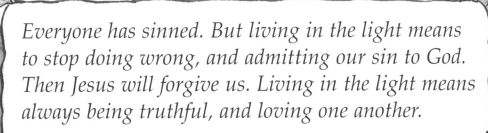

Everyone has sinned. But living in the light means to stop doing wrong, and admitting our sin to God. Then Jesus will forgive us. Living in the light means always being truthful, and loving one another.

As Jesus gave His life for us, we should be willing to give our own lives for another. If we truly love God, we will always give to those in need. Love is not in what we say but what we do, and the way we live.

John taught that God is love. Whoever lives lovingly lives in God, and God lives in them. Perfect love sends away all fear. We show our love for God by obeying His commands.

When John was very old, he was given a special vision from God. God told Him that Jesus was soon going to return to earth. Then he saw heaven. Believers from every nation sang praises around the throne of God.

In the end times, everyone will know that Jesus is Lord.

441

442

John saw a new heaven and a new earth. God and His people were no longer separated. Instead, He lived among them. God Himself dried their tears. There was no more death and no more pain.

God said, "I am making everything beautiful and new!"

He saw a new Jerusalem,
shining like a precious jewel.

It had angels at pearl gates. The city had no
sun or moon, because God was it's light.
There were no lies or tricks. There were no
evil people, only those that loved God.
The river of life flowed through the city.

445

At the end of John's vision, Jesus spoke.
"Listen, I am coming soon! I was in the
beginning, and I will be there at the end."

In the beginning when God created the world, there was total darkness. But when Jesus returns in the end, there will be nothing but light. Jesus is the light of the world. If we let Him into our hearts, His light will shine through us. Someday we shall see Him in heaven, and there we will live in the warm joy of God's love, forever.

447

You have reached the end of the Bible. I hope you'll keep its wisdom close to your heart. May the Word of God guide you as you continue to grow!